Connecting Entrepreneurs, Philanthropists and Influencers.

BUSINESS
BOOSTER TODAY MAGAZINE
THE #1 GERMANY BASED MAGAZINE FOR THE GLOBAL ENTREPRENEUR

THE VERSATILE TESLA X

VOL. 1 | NO.6 |
XMAS 2018

CONTENT

COVER STORY

Test Drive of the Tesla X

By Christian Bartsch

Due to the Diesel Scandal electric Vehicles are getting a better Foothold in the Automotive Market.

1

2

STARTUPS

Business Booster Today

Boosting businesses in L.A.

Orsi B. Nagi

2

2

06	**Power couples turn ideas into a Global Business** Greg JC Granier	24	**Property Sourcing provides Profits around the World** John Stokoe
08	**Turn around Non-Buyers into Happy Clients** Christian Bartsch	26	**Business Growth Fundamentals** Mona Tenjo
10	**Its not about You - Its about Them!** D. & M. Nakovski	28	**What do You do with Your Money?** Kirsti Shapiro
11	**Quickly Enhance the Quality of Your Busy Life** Marina Kotzé		
20	**Creating an Eco-Friendly Automotive Service** Sam Komeha		
22	**Business Booster Today Team is boosting Businesses in LA** Orsi B. Nagy		

CONNECT WITH US

Read more Business Booster Today Magazine content at **BusinessBoosterToday.com**

Download the **Business Booster Today App** for iPhone or Android.

Like the **Business Booster Today Magazine on Facebook** for the latest news, photos, videos and exclusive online content.

Follow **@mybbtmagazine** on Twitter and keep informed on breaking news and busines trends.

View stories and photos on Instagram and get a backstage insight. Follow us at **businessboostertoday**

Make connections with fellow entrepreneurs and business people in our community at businessboostertoday.com

FOUNDERS CORNER

You need to be ahead of the game! Successful entrepreneurs improve their relationships, marketing, negotiation and sales skills.

By Sue Baumgärtner-Bartsch & Christian Bartsch

In business there will always be days that feel cold and hopeless. As an entrepreneur you gradually learn to cope with this roller coaster. You expand your ability to enjoy even the smallest success.

Why is that so important? When you experience a painful or disappointing situation you are able to lift yourself out of a negative mindset much faster. That is why we need to be grateful even for a small positive spark as it may take a considerable amount of patience until we reach the next big success moment in our life.

We all tend to blame our problems to the economy, to politics or even to our enemies. Reality is that when we let such stuff attack us it is our fault. We need to improve our abilities to keep our business afloat at high speed. This does not happen if we just continue to waste our energy on activities that will not help us progress.

If we remain at home we will not be able to expand or business. We need to gain new ideas, insights and even business relationships. You never know when you need the helping hand of another entrepreneur.

If you do not make the effort to connect with people you will not be able to exercise your communication skills. what if you meet a person that wants to buy your service or product? Then you need to exercise your pitch.

Depending on your situation you should not come over like a tape recorder who doesn't even think that the message your are telling is in no way related to your prospect.

Learn to build your marketing profile so that you attract them and give them a good reason to interact with the opportunities you are offering them.

Understand how media credibility and media visibility can help you increase your prices and turnover. You need to know where you want to go in order to recognize the true reason you need to do it this way.

If you need some guidance to take your business to the next level, get in touch with our branding, marketing and business coaches:

https://meetme.so/bbtmag

EDITORIAL TEAM

Christian Bartsch
Publisher & Editor in Chief

Sue Baumgärtner-Bartsch
VP & Interview Editor

Orsi Beata Nagy
Eastern Europe Editor

Hazel Herrington
Africa Editor

John Stokoe
Property Editor

Gábor Dobos
VIP Photographer

Udo Bartsch
Business Editor

Aldrin-David Verburgt
VIP Stylist

Jan Erik Horgen
Norwegian Editor

Greg JC Granier
Fun & Speaking Editor

Gábor Dobos
VIP & Stage Photographer

Eren Ünlü
Technology Editor

IMPRESS

ISSN (Print Edition)
2627-9223

ISSN (Online Edition)
2627-9231

PUBLICATION DATE
20.12.2018

PUBLICATION SERIES INFO
December 2018 No. 6

PUBLICATION REVISION ID
2019-11-26--1

PUBLISHER & EDITOR IN CHIEF
Christian Bartsch

ASSOCIATE EDITOR & VP
Sue Baumgaertner-Bartsch

CONTRIBUTING EDITORS
Udo Bartsch, Hazel Herrington, Jan Erik Horgen, Orsi Beata Nagy, Sylvija Popovic, John Stokoe, Eren Ünlü, Greg JC Granier

CONTRIBUTING WRITERS
Michelle Davis, Hanne Egeberg, Robb Evans, Billy Gajic, Michael Knulst, Marina Kotze, Louis Kotze, Sam Komeha, Janine Jakob, Jaine Lopez, Robert Martin, Michael Bart Mathews, Milos & Danijela Nakovski, Christine Nielsen, Nina Peutherer, Richard Peutherer, Kirstie Shapiro, Tomer Sapir Spitkowski, Mona Tenjo, Janine Van Throo, Brett Yeager, Erwin Wils

PHOTOGRAPHY
Gábor Dobos, Dalibor Kojic

VIP STYLING & MAKEUP
Aldrin-David Verburgt

PUBLISHED BY
ACATO GmbH, 1st. Floor, Theresienhoehe 28, 80339 Munich, Germany

ADVERTISING & SALES
sales@businessboostertoday.com

Phone +49 89 54041070

www.businessboostertoday.com

SUBSCRIPTIONS
Booster club members: annual membership dues include €197 for a regular one-year subscription and €47 for an electronic member subscription. Non-members subscription rate are €97 for an electronic subscription. Change of address notices and subscriptions should be directed to BBT magazine.
Although BBT Magazine maybe quoted with proper attribution, no portion of this publication may be reproduced unless written permission has been obtained from the publisher.
The views expressed in this magazine are those of the authors and might not reflect the official policies of Publisher and its associated organisations.
The editors assume no responsibility for unsolicited manuscripts but will consider all submissions. Contributors' guidelines are available at businessboostertoday.com. Business Booster Today Magazine is a double-blind, peer-reviewed publication.

To order reprints, visit businessboostertoday.com or email info@businessboostertoday.com.

©2018 ACATO GmbH. "Business Booster Today", "Business Booster Today Magazine", "Booster Club", "Booster TV", "Crypto Booster Magazine", "BBT", the Magazine logo and related trademarks, names and logos are the property of ACATO GmbH, and are registered and/or used in Germany, the European Union and countries around the world.

All Content is protected intellectual property and may not reproduced without written consent of the publisher.

GREGTALKS

IDEAS WORST SPREADING

Power couples can turn an idea into a wildly successful global business

By Greg JC Granier

GREGTALKS, IDEAS WORST SPREADING

You read it right it's not ideas **worth spreading**, this one is **TEDtalks slogan**.

If you don't know TED by now, stop reading and get your tablet.

If you do, consider **GREGtalks as a parody of TEDtalks**, where instead of giving you tips to succeed, I am going to give you **tips to fail**, a **kind of reverse psychology** or opposite day, where we eat breakfast for dinner...

There are 3 ways to do things: The right way, the wrong way, or the Greg's way!- Greg Granier

Why? Well, why not? In seminars you hear so many times tips to succeed... and also to think out of the box, so let's do this:

10 TIPS TO FAIL AS AN ENTREPRENEUR

1: ALWAYS HAVE AN EXCUSE.

You started a business and things are not going your way? Well, there is always someone to blame for that, and It's time to track the bad guys instead of wondering what you could do better. The manager, the client, it's PA, gatekeeper, delivery boy, the world works on a different schedule but I paid for my stamp so it's their fault your honour.

2: DON'T INVEST IN YOUR EDUCATION

Look at all the seminars... Why do you think they are for unless scamming you into a world of beliefs that you will never enter unless you pay... No, you learned all you needed to learn in school and as you had good grades you know all about life already. The earth is round, and you will succeed because you have diplomas, what do you need more? Our education system always wants what's best for us.

3: CONSIDER YOUR EMPLOYEES AS WHAT THEY ARE: EMPLOYEES.

Or servants, or slaves... After all, YOU started the company, YOU are the one taking all the risks and they wouldn't be there without you. YOU are more able to say you "kind of" own them. A good leader is not here to form other leaders, he is here to come and conquer!

4: FOLLOW YOUR FAMILY'S ADVICE.

Or your significant other, your siblings, your banker, your tv, your tinder date... The world is full of people that will want to give you advice for your own good because they care! And want the best for you. Your husband is in the right to tell you the seminar you went to is a scam while he spent the day watching football. My mom was super right to tell me to get a job before starting an acting career (haha joke's on you mom, we're in France: there are no jobs)

5: DON'T QUESTION ANYTHING.

If it's on the news it must be true... or on the internet, in books, magazines, and even cereal boxes. Be aware that a certain message is trying to reach you... Some people still think the bible has been written by God himself when he created the world 2000 years ago... And I believe the 10 commandments have been twitted.

6: WAIT UNTIL YOU ARE 1000% READY.

Embrace analysis! After all, you have only one chance so everything needs to be spotlight perfect before launching your new venture. A website, a nice office, an assistant, an assistant for the assistant... Learn by doing? It's for manual people. Clients? They will come eventually...

7 DON'T TOLERATE CRITICISM.

Who said that? I'm going to break their legs.

8: TIME IS MONEY!

And money is time... You are in a loop. Don't take any time for you neither. You will sleep when you're dead, you will work out when you're sick, and you will date when you're retired. Kamasutra for seniors is really trending at the moment, so why waste your good years?

9: TAKE CARE OF BUSINESS MORE THAN YOURSELF

Your business is your baby, and your baby becomes your partner's baby, and your partner becomes your assistant because it's all about the business and we cannot stress this enough!

10: DO NOT HAVE FUN

Fun is for clowns, sarcastic aficionados and stand-up comedians. But I am starting a company so I will not laugh for the next 5 years- I am going to make millions so I need to lose my sense of humour, and Greg jokes all the time so he cannot achieve serious results.

LETS TALK SALES

Turn non-buyers into happy clients

Leads often decline offers but are only lost deals if you do not follow up on them!

By Christian Bartsch

Turning non buyers into clients

In every business there are situations where a lead will decline an offer. This usually is based on a **variety of reasons**. It is the pricing, the product,

the delivery time, the shipping costs, missing functionality, misunderstanding of offer details, general confusion or lack of urgency.

As a business owner and entrepreneur you are the **figure head of sales**. Even if you have a sales team doing all the sales work, you remain the lead sales person. You are the **figure head of your company brand**. Your personal brand and along with it … your values are what make quality leads become buyers and then **lifetime clients**.

The turmoil in life

The life of an entrepreneur is **marked with a success and failure curve** that goes up and down all the time. As you succeed you are happy and even more motivated. When a setback hits you, it **drains more than 3 times the energy** that a success will add to your emotional status.

Having been in business for more than 15 years, I know how you have days you have to battle with people trying to poison your mind and thereby create a negative mind-set in your head. It **drains a lot of energy** to come back up, as in the evening you do not want to go home with negative thoughts and pollute your loved ones mind-set. It is as if you are in a rowing boat and you are going up and down big massive waves. You paddle and paddle. The waves play with your little boat.

In order to escape this rat race you need **to evaluate every presumably lost deal**. If it is not a good deal, then accept this not as a loss but as avoiding the pain of having to manage a bad business arrangement. Should you decide this is a deal worth fighting for you need then to be persistent and get in contact with your lead?

Find the true cause of the decline

Find out why the lead declined your offer. You need to **drill down** to see if the true reason is client confusion or even fear. Some deals are associated with a **considerable economical or legal danger**. If the client cannot allocate a **realistic risk**

measurement to the opportunity, they will make a misinformed decision.

Sometimes it's the price. There are ways to **protect your pricing**. In some cases I even had leads changing their mind and even increasing the deal value. The culture of trying to get discounts is very silly move for many people. You would be astonished for how little of a discount a person will make a purchase. Hence, your persistence can even **get you a better deal**.

Unrealistic expectations

Even an **unrealistic desire** to have extremely fast delivery can lead to an offer being declined. The lead will continue to shop around until they either give up or fall for a false promise of fast delivery. This is where you need to explain to a lead the required time for production, implementation or even the project planning. Cheap and messy product delivery may be fast, but will turn a deal into a nightmare, as the client could be complaining about bugs or setbacks as the development of the desired outcome may take longer. If you client **gains a realistic expectation**, then he will be more willing to **accept your quality approach** as it will save the client a lot of money and headaches in the long run.

Shipping costs you the deal

Could you imagine that a client will decline your offer due to the cost of shipping? Leads **underestimate** the weight and current shipping costs. If a product has a certain weight or size, this can increase the cost of sea, land and air freight. Do not expect your leads to have a realistic understanding of shipping procedures or important transport requirements. Make it easy for them to understand the core issues.

There are plenty of clients who even **ignore import tax costs**. As a business owner you can deduct a certain amount of import costs from your tax payments you owe to your local tax authority. I have been importing and exporting goods to/from a variety of countries. Therefore my business is registered inside Europe with its European import ID. This speeds up the shipments that go into our region as the customs authorities know what we usually import and who we are. If you do not import or export a lot, you do not need this.

Nevertheless, some clients **do not calculate into their purchasing expenses** such costs. If the import declaration is based on massively incorrect figures, it can become a tax issue. Imports from china do tend to become an issue once the local customs authority notices this supplier's **incorrect declarations**. Then they can go after every local client. This is something you can highlight to your lead should you be confronted with a competitors offer that is clearly in violation of the import regulations. Your lead should be honest enough to recognize your warning and prefer to purchase your safer offer.

Turn objections into complaints

When you are handling objections you need to set them aside as **complaints** and continue towards closing the deal. Nevertheless, you need to **identify the true reason** behind this lead's statements.

Wrong product - Right deal

Is the lead looking for a functionality it believes to be missing in your product? Maybe this functionality has a different name or is even obsolete as your product is more advanced and does not need this old feature.

You have to check even if the lead is actually **looking at the wrong product**. You will find a better fitting

solution and if you keep up the game, you will close him there.

Drive around a no money excuse

If you encounter an excuse that they have their card maxed out then you can offer them a payment plan or even go the test route. In 70% of cases you will close the deal there. The other 25% needs more patience. The other 5% are just not the right client for your required budget.

Not your problem

What do you do if your client is so confused that it is not your fault but actually other problems the lead currently has to handle? Then you need even **more patience** during your conversation. You might even be able to resolve the issue for them, and then move directly on to the closing of the deal. I turned many non-buyers during 30 to 60 minute phone calls into **happy clients**. So can you!

Only close deals that are good for your clients and yourself. If you help your clients be successful, then you will be successful in gaining a beneficial reward. Do not undervalue yourself or your products. **Believe in your offers!** ✒

IT'S NOT ABOUT YOU

IT'S ABOUT THEM

By Milos & Danijela Nakovski

Have you ever wondered what make a sales person Great? Have you ever considered when you buy or sell your house that not everyone could be the right realtor for you?

Sometimes, you meet those realtors that simply are out to make a deal, but are not really interested in your concerns and in you as a person. Here is where you can be a game changer in your industry of real estate. But that does not only go for real estate industry.

What makes a great salesperson great at sales is that he or she is wholeheartedly interested in the other person!

Great realtor's true worth is determined by how much more they give in value than they take in payment! - Danijela Nakovski

Selling is really serving greatly your client while giving your time, knowledge and attention to them. Focusing on your client and always striving to add value to other person's life is what sales is all about.

Of course, just by being a human, we are all ultimately driven by self-interest-it's an essential part of human nature. Therefore, we are not suggesting you put your own interest completely on the side, we are saying you should create a value for others for a self-contained reward and satisfaction of knowing you were able to serve. You give because it is who you are.

Here are 5 simple ways that **can create that extra value** and give the **exceptional service** to your clients.

1. Excellence - Be excellent in all tasks you do – How do you greet people on the phone? How do you answer your emails? How do you dress? Do you pay attention how you pronounce your client's name? A great sales person is not doing enough to get paid-they want to see how much more value they can create than what they are paid for! That translates into EXELLENCE!

2.Attention – Do you pay attention to details? Do you listen to your client's needs? Paying attention to what your client wants and needs will definitely create the extra value!

3.Consistency- Be the consistency in this world full of uncertainty. **Make people aware** that they can always count on you to deliver the same quality of service, no matter what! When you combine excellence and consistency you create truly exceptional value!

4.Empathy – Do you put yourself in your client's shows? Do you show them you understand their situation and you are there to hold their hand through the process of the real estate transaction?

5.Appreciation – One of the most powerful ways you can create value for people is simply to appreciate them! Notice the small things they do that make a difference and point them out. Say Thank you and mean it- Treat people with respect and you will create great network around you!

Make the transaction an unforgettable experience for your client!

Danijela's past experience in a corporate communication world, passion in relationship coaching and Milos's experience in sales and negotiations came together beautifully in their real estate carriers.

YOUR BUSY LIFE

How to Quickly Enhance the Quality of Your Busy Life

By Marina Kotze

End of year stress

Nearing the end of the year, business owners and executives often experience increased levels of pressure and stress. Goals for the year need to be reached; physical and mental fatigue, and even burn-out, are commonly at the order of the day; workloads increase and hardly seem to get reduced. Social and family demands also have its toll, as arrangements for upcoming year-end functions have to be made, as well as for the nearing holiday and festive season. The heat is on – from all sides – and energy levels seem to be at an all-time low… Are these familiar descriptions – something you can relate with at this time of the year? Perhaps you may think that these kinds of stressors are something you can associate with all year round, or at least during some specific times of the year.

Take self care seriously

I often emphasise the importance of self-care in all aspects of a person's life. Coping with the intense demands of the business world is extremely important for one's health and wellbeing in the long haul of the business and work journey. Often businesses fail due to the simple fact that business owners are unable to cope with the demands placed on either themselves, the business itself, or both.

> **"Stress is not the biggest killer of our time – but rather our *inability* and *lack of skill* to cope with stress and the demands of this modern era."** – Marina Kotzé

It is of pivotal importance that every time you experience increased levels of stress, you ask yourself, "How am I dealing with this (identify and name stressor) right now?"

Take time to reflect

Being quiet for a few minutes, investing in your "thinking time" and asking yourself this one simple question, will immediately increase your self-awareness and activate certain areas of your brain for effective problem solving. Your frame of mind will be towards **looking for solutions**, which, in turn, will enhance the quality of your internal levels of motivation, resulting in action steps towards the right direction for a positive outcome.

Referring to the quality of life of the busy business owner and executive, it is of crucial importance to maintain one's level of happiness. Yes, happiness in life is a precious gift to us and it is our responsibility to look after it. Happiness can – and should – be experienced even during immensely stressful times.

Laughter is a great healer

Happiness is a choice and fortunately there are some tools we can use to activate happiness in our lives. **One of these tools is *laughter*.** I would like to introduce laughter to you as a simple, yet highly effective, tool to quickly **enhance the quality of your busy life**. Did you know that babies and young children laugh an average of 300 times per day? Sadly, in adults, this statistic is drastically reduced to a mere 17 times per day. Humans are born to naturally laugh, but throughout life we lose and "unlearn" that innate ability. Laughter is our natural stress antidote and **drastically increases our quality of life** as one experiences the many health benefits of laughter.

This article should stimulate your curiosity about laughter as a means to increase your levels of happiness and, in the follow-up article to this one, I will elaborate on more specific facts and techniques about laughter.

AHEAD OF TIME

The Tesla X is an amazing power house

By Christian Bartsch

If you have been confronted with the consequences of the Diesel scandal then you will have had to rethink your future plans for purchasing vehicles.

As an entrepreneur you have set your mind to **create a legacy with the business ventures** you are working on. Polluting the environment and hurting the people you love is definitely **not in alignment with legacy**.

Don't be short sighted

Short sightedness of some car manufacturers and suppliers has led to innovation being labels as evil. There are people out there who would love us to go back to horse carts. Reality teaches us that this **utopia is just not realistic**.

Hence, as business owners we need to re-evaluate our car pool and the future way of acquiring vehicles. It does not matter if you are in favour of leasing or purchasing new or second hand vehicles for your company.

You have to **realign your mobility to your legacy goals**.

The problematic issues caused by the diesel manipulation are also hitting the unleaded petrol dependant vehicles. Being critical in your selection of the engine you want to have in your vehicles must not be taken light.

What if you purchase a brand new vehicle and then you cannot drive into a major city? In Germany big cities are being **forced by court orders** to keep diesel vehicles outside their boundaries.

Why should we purchase a state sponsored new diesel vehicle when one major city after the next is being **forced to prohibit these new diesel vehicles** to enter their areas?

For an entrepreneur who is in the future, this kind of offers make absolutely no sense. It will only take a few years till we see the same happening to the combustion vehicles that do not use diesel.

Electrical vehicles are sprinting

The only sensible action for a business is to look towards electric vehicles. If you think this is only something for small cars then you are wrong. The German parcel service teamed up with a **German Start-up to mass produce postal delivery** vehicles. They are massively replacing their sprinter vehicles with these efficient commercial cars. They joint venture is so successful that other companies have started ordering from that start-up delivery vehicles for their own car pool.

When we look at the market for electric cars we need to **look at efficiency, quality and forward thinking abilities** of the individual teams. Many of the old school vehicle manufacturers are putting out electric vehicles that are *not exactly beautifully looking*. They remind us more of plastic toys.

Safety first

That takes us to the feeling if this kind of vehicles can be safe on the roads. Recently the London police had a car accident. Its BMW i3 had an accident. The police vehicle had been **smashed severely**. The risk of police vehicles being involved in small or large accidents are much higher that of regular vehicle drivers. Well, the true reason is that most of us do not drive at high speed through a congested city. When police officers travel through our cities **at high speed** to protect their citizens against evil people then they have to be fast.

Age is no measurement

When you look at the newcomer Tesla then you will notice that you do not need to be 100 years old to design and release forward thinking vehicles that are safe. The amount of serious vehicle accident fatalities is much higher with the other brands. Tesla has been focusing on safety and innovation.

Tesla vehicles always up-to-date

Even their **ability to update all**

vehicles every 2 weeks without having to get the car into their service stations is way ahead of its competitors. It does not matter if we take an Audi, BMW or VW to your service station, you will not get your firmware updated if your vehicle is very old. My BMW 5er series can get updates for its navigation system. That only includes maps but no functionality.

I am stuck with a diesel vehicle that cannot be updated. Its radio system, its wiper settings, its motor settings, and other functionalities will get no updates. I am stuck with outdated media entertainment? That's something Tesla gets fixed in no time. Maybe I should look at **what Tesla has to offer**?

Our Tesla X Experience

Recently we visited the Tesla showroom in Munich. The service and approach to new leads is an attractive way of thinking. When you take the Tesla X for a ride you will be astonished.

Yes, Tesla develops its vehicle portfolio year by year. Two years ago I tested the Tesla S model and now sitting at the weal of the Tesla X you notice the **continuous innovation** happening at Tesla.

The driving experience is so unique I can imagine how we will be travelling in future. Yes, there are other competitors closing up, but they are missing a unique competitive advantage.

Leadership is the key to success

They do not have the **figure head Elon Musk**. Having an empowering and forward pushing leader like Elon Musk at the wheel of this brand is so vital. Elon **attracts some of the best engineers** who are capable of changing the way we are travelling. The disputes with the SEC do not make a difference to Tesla's innovation. It is only a stepping stone for the business and its leader to further mature.

They are so disruptive that even state sponsored companies from china have a difficulty in entering the selective niche of Tesla. Tesla is offering now 3 different models to provide access to their technology for 3 different sections of the society.

The Model 3 is their newest vehicle looking towards the middle class vehicle section. For many business owners the Tesla S has become a **statement of life style**. Nevertheless, the Tesla X has its place on our roads.

Gain your space travelling

If you travel with up to 7 people you need space. Those of you who represent your businesses at shows and exhibitions you might need to take roll-ups and other equipment you cannot ship with a parcel service. You need space. This is where usually a fast and versatile luxury vehicle is great.

Compare the alternatives

At the present if you want to move from a BMW 5er touring or Mercedes E300 you need to accept the fact that the old school manufacturers have nothing electric on offer at the moment. So you will want to look at the Tesla X. Its transport space can be **up to 2000 litres**.

That is more than a 5er touring. When you look at the weight of a 5er Touring and a Tesla X then you will notice these are heavy vehicles. Nevertheless the Tesla x is **efficient and stable** on the road.

Speed and comfort

When you press down the accelerator you will be astonished at the massive speed and power its power train can push the vehicle forward. Now you need to keep in mind the Tesla X comes as **4 wheel drive**. So you have the **power and stability** of 4 individually monitored wheels.

Whether you cruse along a motor way or you are travelling in a heavy congested city, the driving **experience is so wonderful**. You could imagine this like the effects of meditations. No hectic and when needed the Tesla X will turbo boost you faster than a combustion engine.

You can select **3 different battery configurations**. From the 75 to the P100D ... you have great choice. You can be sure that the sales people

will ask you the right questions to guide you to the ideal configuration. This excellent client focus makes Tesla a unique brand already working on its own long lasting legacy.

Seating is wellness on 4 wheels

The seating is available as a 5 and 7 seater configuration. Both settings allow you to fold the back seats down so you can turn this awesome vehicle into a transport miracle. You can **gain so much space** that you could never get with a competitors diesel vehicle. Even under the front bonnet you will have additional space for luggage.

Stylish cockpit with great view

The new **cockpit layout** of the Tesla X is so **beautifully designed** that it fully aligns with the big screen in the middle of the cockpit. As you see in our pictures, the front windscreen is so big. It provides an **unrivalled view** range. It sun protection ensures you are <u>not blinded</u> by a sun that comes in from far above.

The sun blind is <u>cleverly hidden</u> on the side above the front doors. You just move it to the front where you need it. You can even fold down an **extra protective flap**. If you need to have it covering the front area, it even has a clever system that locks the sun blind into the side of the front mirror holder.

Enjoy clean air in the Tesla X

If you suffer of an allergy then you will notice how clean the air is in a Tesla X. The built in HEPA air ventilation filters are of the **high standards** used in modern clinics. Therefore the **air quality is so refreshing** when you compare it with other vehicles when you drive through a congested and polluted city.

Music as pure as it can be

The Tesla X comes with quite an impressive sound system. You can listen to your favourite music via their entertainment system that connects music sources from the internet. With its over 17 loud speakers Tesla can ramp up your joy

of listening to music.

As the interior of the Tesla X is very quiet, you can enjoy the music quality at all different levels of intensity.

Automatic front doors

When you want to get in or out, the doors are aware of obstacle and try to *avoid getting the paint work of the front doors damaged*. Even the back doors can be **operated just by pressing the button** on the side column. No more heavy door lifting or swiping or pushing.

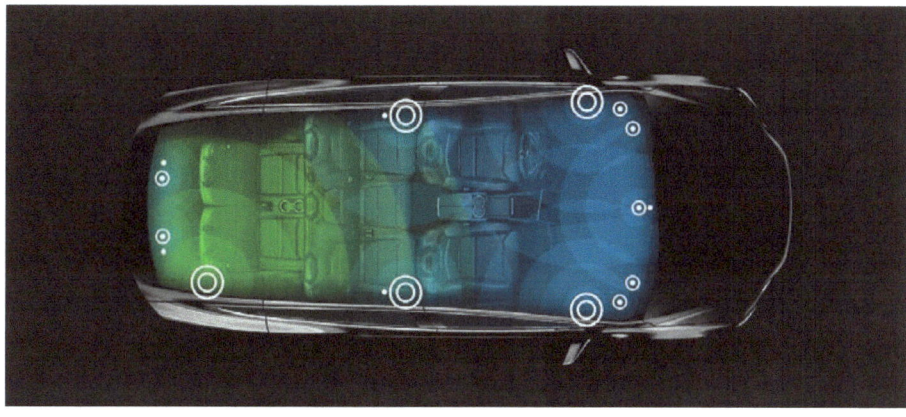

Fall in love with the Tesla X

This ease of usage makes Tesla a **perfect match for busy entrepreneurs** who have no time to sit around in a work shop to get their vehicle updated. Did you know, you can set the height of your seat to match your GPS location?

Yes, you can set the seat to lower down when you drive onto your property grounds and to be higher when you are driving around the city. Combine this with the multiple parking cameras.

When we tried the parking features of the Tesla X we were **truly amazed how well it coped** with this rather difficult parking spot. It was very narrow. We only had to help with the last bit since it was an extremely narrow spot.

Who drives Tesla is ahead

Is Tesla only something for nerds? Only for men? No, Tesla is a brand that provides awesome cars for men and women who want to have a **totally different experience**.

The forward thinking abilities of these vehicles are so ahead of the competition, that when **autonomous driving** will be legalized in different countries the vehicles only need to **get an update** and then will be able to provide this safe and convenient assistance.

Other cars have no chance to be updated. Isn't it **environmentally friendly** to be able to update older

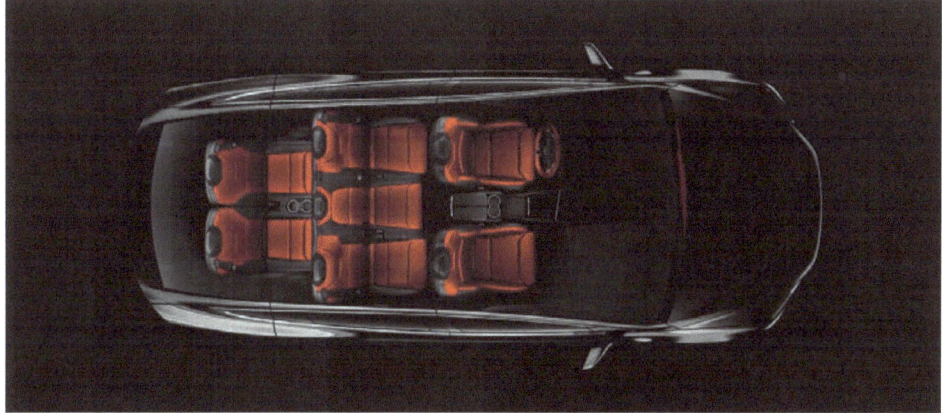

Fast updating route maps

The map functionality is so nice to read and updates by far faster than in older versions of their software. Tesla uses google maps with the Navigon technology to provide up to date maps.

You can even set their air settings for **front and back seating** areas. In other cars you need to use old style turn wheels or buttons to set your seat heating. With Tesla this happens over the front display screen. If you have a full seat heating configuration then you can set the **heat for all 5 to 7 seats** individually. Even if Tesla comes up with a new settings configuration, your vehicle will get the update without you having to fiddle around with an update.

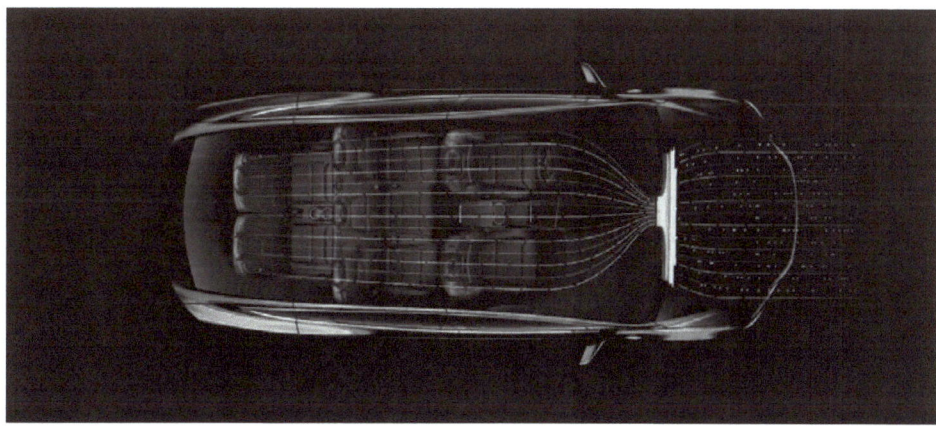

vehicles?

Interior and exterior designs

Tesla does not have a large amount of colours. They have a well arranged selection. Their interior uses special artificial leather that **does not get stained**.

I have to take my BMW every year to get a special leather treatment when I wear my favourite jeans. With Tesla seats, I do not have this problem. I just take a wet cloth and wipe over the seat and the **stains are gone**.

If I travel a lot I even have to take my car twice a year to the shop. Once I got a horrible orange stain in my boot due to a badly packed Indian take away. The stain still remains. With Tesla this would have not been an issue.

The **time and money I save through Tesla's seating** is massive. Doing business around the world requires a lot of travelling. I want to use my leisure time to spend it with my family and not in a work shop or travelling back and forward to get my car cleaned.

Range of electric cars

Of course you might claim that the travel range of an electric vehicle is small. To be honest, you should **have a break** every 2 hours. That is the recommended time frame that automotive clubs and the police suggest to avoid accidents.

So what does it matter if you are having a walk to **stretch your legs** and have some food while your car gets a refreshment for its own batteries? There are so many charging stations across North America, Europe and Asia.

Tesla is expanding its **fast charging** stations across Eastern Europe. So if you need to drive to countries such as **Croatia, Slovakia, Poland** or even Russia, you will have no issues with charging up your vehicle.

A great brand association

Did you know that one of the most **influential inventors** was called *Nikola Tesla*? Yes, he came from Croatia and created a multitude of inventions we take for granted today. Nikola Tesla moved to **New York in 1884**.

With hardly any money he embarked on a life journey to develop electrical solutions that make our life easier.

It is such a fitting coincidence that the car manufacturer has the name Tesla as its brand name.

Innovators are regularly confronted with non-believers and haters that do not want them to succeed. Nikola Tesla **succeeded against all odds** to provide us with wonderful innovations.

Elon Musk has to battle with other kinds of obstacles. He never gives up and that is why we can enjoy today the driving experience of the Tesla X.

Fly high with innovative wings

You might have noticed the **wig doors that fold up** for the back seats. When you sit in the back of the Tesla X you will see that you have additional natural lighting. The doors **can cope with narrow parking** conditions.

If you have to strap children into their safety seats, these folding doors make it **much easier** to get the kids belted up. We do not need to turn our bodies in an awkward way to get them arranged. The Tesla X model is the **dream car** for parents.

Elon has as father himself experienced the issues of travelling with kids. His **passion to change** the way we travel has no boundaries. He has made it much easier. Well, you might point at sliding doors of other manufacturers.

Nevertheless, these sliding doors do not give you the head space you need to get to the inner side of the children seats. Tesla has even for this space. Why should you want something else? Wing doors are an **awesome futuristic reality**.

Price tag vs. value delivered

You might say he price tag of a Tesla X is far too high. Just go to the configuration app of comparable diesel vehicles. You will be astonished to find that **the competition will ask you to pay far more** for a vehicle that is not fully ahead of its time.

The Tesla x selling above EUR 90.000 is therefore not really an expensive vehicle when you look at the value and competitive advantages it provides to you. Do not look at a car with the eye of a consumer.

You are an entrepreneur. Look at its value and price stability. When you buy an iPhone you do not compare its price tag with that of a galaxy phone. The iPhone is a product of its own in its own nice. The same applies to the Tesla product range.

The Tesla market value is stable

Even if you decide to sell your Tesla in 2-5 years the value will not drop as massively as with the diesel vehicles. Tesla is so flexible that it will help you switch from an old diesel vehicle to an environmentally friendly vehicle. This is conveniently set up that it is difficult to resist their offers.

Experience the Tesla X

The Tesla X has so much to offer that you need to experience this vehicle. You will notice that driving it is so cool that you do not have a slow car. The Tesla vehicles have more than 400 horse power to offer. Since we do not speed at 200km / hour we do not need this force, but if you need to overtake in a critical situation, the Tesla X with its nearly 2.5 tons accelerates like a rocket. This is no slow turtle. It is a power house of its own.

If you are an action taker then you need to go to meet the Tesla X in your nearby Tesla dealership. Charge up your life with a new kind of power! It will ramp up your legacy. ↗

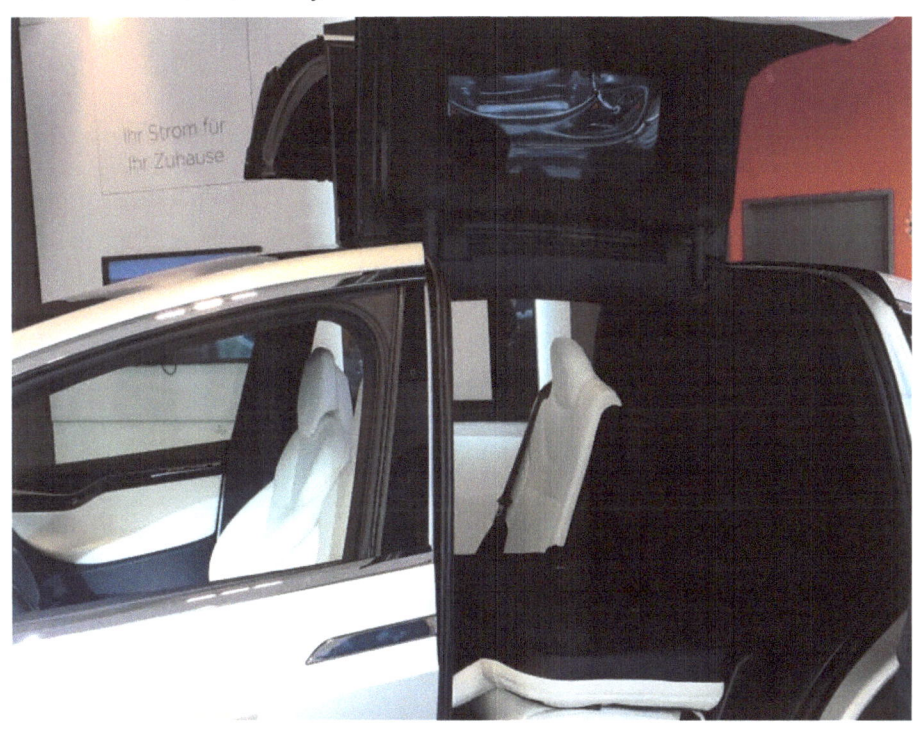

ECO-FRIENDLY

Creating an Eco-Friendly Automotive Service Center

By Sam Komeha

The picturesque region of Piedmont in northwest Italy, bordering France in the west and Switzerland in the north, is one of the richest regions in Italy. The regions capital, Turin, has been home to no less than 37 motor companies, including the sports car brand Abarth and legendary designer Pininfarina.

In automotive service centers, attracting new customers and retaining old ones is incredibly important. While there are many factors that go into how customers are found and kept, an **automotive service center's public image** is one of the most important factors. One of the **key factors** to improve a service center's **image of quality and care** is by taking an **interest** in the things that are **important to customers**.

In a time where pollution and environmental hazards are growing at alarming rates, many customers are choosing to spend their hard-earned money at businesses who show an active interest in preserving the environment.

From shops that have sworn off plastic bags to coffee shops that don't use straws or reusable cups, businesses who take an interest in reducing their environmental impact are seeing positive returns in the form of profits and better public opinion.

Though it may seem like a difficult task, there is no reason that service centers can't take steps toward becoming **eco-friendlier**, and, in the process, attract a larger, more environmentally conscious customer base.

But, with all the different byproducts of the service industry, how is it possible for a service center to **become more environmentally friendly**? The answer lies in a few different, relatively easy, steps.

Service centers who are dedicated to reducing the amount of harm they do to the environment will be able to turn their service center into an **environmentalist's dream** in less time, and with less effort, than they ever thought possible.

Dispose of Waste Materials Properly

Batteries, fluids, tires, metal drums, and many other products are disposed of every day in service centers. While there is no way around using these materials, service centers can dispose of these materials responsibly to work toward being eco-friendly. Finding a local recycling company and ensuring that materials aren't disposed of in a hazardous way will help the service center protect the environment.

Team Up with Environmentalist Groups

Many dealerships team up with causes or charities throughout the year to **raise awareness** and help a great cause. Businesses looking to be eco-friendly should consider working with a cause or charity that helps the environment. Planting a tree for each car serviced, employees volunteering their time to clean up trash locally, or holding a recycling event will **help the service center** improve the environment and attract eco-conscious patrons. Every customer will feel better spending their money with an **environmentally friendly company**.

Limit Usage of Single-Use Products

Single-use products are one of the biggest contributors to the current

AUTO SERVICE

trash problem. By creating a service center that uses as few single-use products as possible, daily operations will have a much smaller negative impact on the environment. For daily service operations, buying fluids in bulk rather than smaller containers, using reusable service tags rather than paper disposables, and using rags instead of paper shop towels, when possible, will go a long way to reducing waste. For employees, eliminating single-use coffee maker pods, disposable cups, and plastic water bottles will help to contribute to environmentally friendly practices.

Save the Environment and Attract New Customers

Since the environment is a cause that most people care about, becoming eco-friendly is a great business move. These simple changes will allow service centers to market themselves as eco-friendly, which will attract customers and increase the public's opinion of the business. Once service centers take these easy steps to help save the environment, they'll wonder why they didn't start their environmentalist efforts sooner.

BUSINESS BOOSTER TODAY TEAM IS BOOSTING BUSINESS IN LOS ANGELES

By Orsi Beata Nagy

The great Gathering

Every entrepreneur and business owner **from around the globe** were waiting for the 5th November to come just like a child is waiting for Christmas. If you have ever been to a Mega Success then you know what I am talking about.

If not, it might seem like an exaggeration however if you want to spend 6 days amongst business people, millionaires, billionaires from **75 countries**, meet them, build your **relational capital**, **do business** internationally or **interview celebrities** then Mega Success is the place to be in every November.

The meeting point Mega Success

Mega Success is an annual event in USA, organized by the JT Foxx Organization where business owners, coaches and celebrities get together to celebrate success, learn from each other and network to elevate their business further.

It is about everything that a business owner can do and probably should do, starting from being fit, learn about new technologies and opportunities to just simply network.

I personally walked away with several **new clients**, some **potential clients**, managed to brand my businesses and equally myself, personally **meet celebrities** while having fun at the same time. Sounds cool, right? It is more than just cool, this is the event you must experience at least once in your lifetime.

Well represented in L.A.

Business Booster Today was well represented in **Los Angeles** by many of the editorial members of our global team and we also had a chance to meet in person from all continents. We supported **Vikas Malkani,** the World's #1 Wisdom and Wealth Coach, who is on the cover of Business Booster Today (Vol.1 No.3.).

He delivered an amazing speech on the Intelligent Millionaires Network's LA Chapter and we sold out the hard copies of the magazine before Mega Success even started.

The lead-magnetic Magazine

During Mega Success we had an amazing turnout for our stand and also for the competitions Business Booster Today had for the attendees of the event. Participants had a chance to **win some amazing prices** like being featured in the magazine.

The USP - Quality Content

Most importantly we have received amazing feedbacks about the **quality** of Business Booster Today's **content** which ensured us that we are on the right path to reach **20 million people globally to inspire, educate and empower them to grow and explode their businesses.**

I personally was amazed on the feedback on **my article** *"Do You Have A Business Or Just Another Job?"* which was published in Vol.1. No.5. issue.

Imagine that 2500 people attended the event and people were flooding to me **not just complimenting but having a discussion** on how they can improve on themselves and on their businesses as well. This is a great example showing you that branding does work, which is one of **our key goals at Business Booster Today** to assist you reaching global branding.

PROPERTY ...

By John Stokoe

It's well known that investing on property provides solid returns and financial security for many people around the world. Potentially the most important factor in generating these returns is an education.

A lack of education can be devastatingly costly in an investment and a lack of education is also the reason why many feel they may not have enough funds to profit in the industry. That's where they are wrong.

It's well known that investing on property provides solid returns and financial security for many people around the world. Potentially the most important factor in generating these returns is an education. A lack of education can be devastatingly costly in an investment and a lack of education is also the reason why many feel they may not have enough funds to profit in the industry. That's where they are wrong.

Put simply, property sourcing is the process of finding, negotiating, and 'packaging-up' property-related business opportunities or 'deals', to sell on to investors for a fee.

A property 'deal' is simply a pre-negotiated agreement with a vendor, who has agreed to sell their property at a negotiated price. As a sourcing agent, your job is to package this deal into an investment grade opportunity and sell it on to investors.

In the UK for example, these opportunities are typically sold for between £2,000 and £5,000 per deal, so just one deal a month could comfortably replace the income or salary of most 9-5 jobs—with far less time invested!

When starting out, a realistic expectation is that you could expect to secure a deal for every 20 properties you view. As you get more experienced this will improve to 1 in 10, or even less. So, simple maths says that if you view 10 houses a week (which is achievable even when doing this part-time) you should see 40 properties in a month, which would result in 2 deals. At an average of £3,000 per deal, that's a possible £6,000 income per month from property sourcing.

The beauty of property sourcing is that you can, very quickly generate large sums of monthly income without even owning a property, by leveraging market mechanics and becoming an intermediary between buyer and seller. At the lower end, property sourcing can make you £3000-6000 per month, but when systematised for volume, some people are sourcing upwards of 4 deals a month making in the region of £12,000, and that's before even considering the experienced sourcing agents trading commercial and land opportunities. At the upper end of sourcing, some agents are making in the region of £50,000 on single development deals where an investor can build 50-100+ houses! That's a little way off for those just starting out, but the point is… the sky is the limit.

Property is a reliable and robust wealth building strategy relied upon for decades. The reality is that many investors are cash rich and time poor. They want to invest in property, but lack either the time or expertise required to find and secure 'investment grade' property deals themselves. They are, however, willing to pay a sizeable fee for the opportunities to be packaged and

SOURCING PROFITS

delivered to them.

There are three main reasons why investors utilize sourcing agents:

· **Time**

Some investors simply don't have the time to invest in finding and securing new property deals, so instead they partner with a sourcing agent who can do that on their behalf.

· **Expertise**

For some investors it's about expertise. Many landlords are not professionally trained and therefore lack the skills required to build systems and processes that consistently produce high-value property deals. By partnering with a sourcing agent, they're able to leverage the agent's education and expertise to secure property deals which they may otherwise be unable to access; such as off-market and direct-to-vendor opportunities.

· **Area Knowledge**

Finally, for some investors, partnering with a sourcing agent is simply about accessing different investment areas with the least amount of effort. Time is money, and some savvy investors would rather partner with a sourcing agent and pay a fee for each opportunity, than invest the time in travelling to and understanding a new town or city. By leveraging the expertise of a sourcing agent, investors are able to capitalise on the agent's local knowledge & network.

Come back next month and I'll go through the 1st of 5 easy steps on how to generate profits from sourcing property.

If this interest's you and you would like to know more beforehand then please visit

www.sourcemyproperty.com/contact/

BUSINESS GROWTH

Setting the right market prices with Bowman's Strategy Clock

By Mona Tenjo

Do you know which options you have to position yourself price-wise? In this fourth part of the Business Growth Fundamentals Series, we will take a look at Bowman's Strategy Clock.

Bowman's Strategy Clock is a model developed by Cliff Bowman and David Faulkner. It is an extension of Porter's competitive strategy model which only looked at three basic strategies. Bowman's Strategy Clock refined 8 strategies to differentiate yourself within competition.

The model is built like a clock which considers two dimensions:

· Perceived value to the customer

· Price

This clock tells you if your customers will be **willing to buy your product** or what you can do **to be competitive again.**

Let's review the 8 strategies:

Strategy 1: Low price and low perceived value. This is a strategy of pure price war. Customers of these products will always buy from the cheapest provider. If you are cheaper than the others, you can survive on this strategy. But you always have to expect that somebody else shows up who is cheaper than you.

Strategy 2: Low price and medium perceived value. This is the most common strategy in the retail market. You still compete on prices, but the customer perceives the value of the good better than in strategy 1.

Strategy 3: This strategy is called

WANT TO INCREASE YOUR PROFIT MARGIN? ADD VALUE TO YOUR PRODUCT AND GET BRANDED!

FUNDAMENTALS

Hybrid model. This strategy is based on a high perceived value to the customer but a low price. A typical example for this strategy is IKEA.

Strategy 4: The fourth strategy is called **"Differentiation"**. Customers perceive a very high value and you charge a medium price for it. An example for this strategy is Starbucks. Starbucks is differentiated, so they don't just sell regular coffee. They created an environment around the coffee, you can sit there, you can work there. They are definitely more expensive than simply buying your coffee at a grocery store.

Strategy 5: This strategy is called **"Focused Differentiation".** Customers perceive high value from the good and the good is expensive. This is the **typical luxury good area** with **brands like Luis Vuitton**, Gucci, Ferrari, Patek Philippe just to name a few. Here, people don't care how much it costs. They feel so much value from the product**, they will pay any price** they want.

The following strategies 6, 7 and 8 are risky strategies. Let's check out why.

Strategy 6: This strategy is called "**Risky High Margins**". That means you still have a **very high price, but the customer doesn't really perceive the value anymore.** That is a risky strategy, because you don't know how long clients are still going to be willing to pay for your product at this price point. If customers don't perceive the value, then it is just a matter of time until a competitor is going to win your clients. That is why this is risky. You can earn a lot of money if you have clients, but if you have some kind of substitute or some other competitor joining the game, you may lose your business.

Strategy 7: This strategy consists of a **high price and a low value**. You can only survive here, if you are a monopoly. Having a low value for a high price may be the death of your company. Only monopolies can survive such a setting.

Strategy 8: This strategy is called "**Loss in Market Share**". Your product has a **medium price but a low perceived value.** In this strategy, differentiation is missing. An example for this strategy would be Tesco in the last few years. They have suffered pretty significant market share losses. Either you have to increase the perceived value to go up to Differentiation or you have to lower the price. So that are the options they have.

How to apply this model to your business?

1. Identify where you are located on the clock

2. If you are in the "risk zone", you need to get out there as fast as possible. Either increase the perceived value, add more benefits for the customer, increase your quality, brand yourself or reduce your price.

3. If you are in any other segment, check if you are happy with where you are located. If not, try **to increase the perceived value** or **differentiate yourself** in order to increase your prices.

Apply this to your business! Assess where you are standing. Look at what you do and what strategies you have available, especially regarding product pricing. ↗

Mona Tenjo is the creator of RespectStrategy, a strategic management consultancy that helps enterprises to identify where profit and efficiency is lost and fixes it. The focus is on the areas of Strategic Management, Communication Structures, People, and Systems.

WHAT DO YOU DO WITH YOUR MONEY?

Save it, spend it, or invest it?

By Kirstie Shapiro

Banks and Buildings

Banks may be a relatively safe place to keep your money, however with interest rates at an all-time low, they most certainly are not a favored place to stash your extra cash. The question then, is, were can you put your savings?

The Bank of England recently raised their interest rates from 0.5 to 0.75%, although better than before, 0.75% doesn't give you much after a year's saving. For every £100 you leave sitting in your savings account, you only get an extra 75p a year!!

With that being said, it has to be brought to your attention, that although interest rates are up by 0.25% and if you have a tracker rate mortgage, the interest rate on that will have or will shortly be rising by 0.25%, however, although interest rates on savings account should rise, they may well not necessarily rise by the full 0.25%.

Why does the Bank of England increase and decrease the interest rates?

When the Banks decrease the interest rate, the objective is to try to get people to spend more money. When mortgage payments are lower, people have a little bit more spare money at the end of the month, and if interest rates are also low, then people can't see any point in saving it and therefore are inclined to go out and spend it. The advantage for the Bank is that when people are out spending their spare cash, it helps to boost the economy.

With the rise in interest rates at this time in the UK, it is a wonder what the Banks are really up to. Although an increase of a quarter percent won't cause most people to be on the bread-line, it does add to financial pressures, especially at this time with the outcome of Brexit being so uncertain. For savers, an increase like this, of 0.25%, is not something to rave about from the roof tops, in reality, inflation continues to erode people's money at a faster rate than the interest rate can bump up their savings.

You can't save it, you can't spend it, so what shall you do with it?

If you have savings, the question now is, should you continue to keep it in the bank, and if not, what is there to do with this spare money?

The first thing to do is actually discover the difference between saving and investing. When we save money, the idea is to put money aside a little at a time. Usually you save in order to purchase something specific such was a holiday, or a car. Savings can also be put aside as "rainy-day funds", to cover for unseen costs or emergencies that may arise from time to time, like a broken boiler.

Savings are put into cash products such as savings accounts at a bank or building society. On the other hand, investing is when you take your money and put it into a product or

service with the intention of making that money grow, because of an increase in its value. Examples of different types of investments are stocks, property or shares in a company or fund.

How do you know if you are ready to invest?

The first criteria to consider when taking on an investment strategy is to look at your financial goal. Are your financial goals short term, medium term or are they long term?

Short term goals, can be viewed as things you intend to do within the next five years. Medium term goals can be described as things that you intend to do within the next five to ten years, while longer term goals are for things you won't need the money for, for ten years or more. It is also very dependent on how much money you currently have available to work with which will determine whether or not investment is for you right now.

For medium to longer term goals it is prudent to invest as inflation can very seriously affect the value of your cash savings over time.

The stock market very often does much better than cash products over the long term, which provides a chance for greater returns and being higher risk, also for greater losses. Company shares, is another long-term strategy that can be very lucrative, once more, this comes with a higher risk, and therefore the chance of a higher return on investment.

Real estate or property investment comes in two packages: direct and indirect property investment. Here we are going to investigate these two types of investment in greater detail.

Direct Property Investment

A direct property investment includes things like buy-to-let, which pretty much is exactly what it sounds like, you buy a property and you rent it out to tenants in order to make a profit on your investment.

You will know that this type of investment strategy is right for you, if you prefer to invest in something that feels more tangible than stocks and shares. It is important to keep in mind that this sort of investment is a long-term investment as property prices can fluctuate quite considerably over a ten-year period.

There is also always the risk that you may not in fact earn a profit on your investment, due to the costs involved, such as mortgages or other money borrowing and the costs of running a property. Getting involved in buy-to-let also means that you then

become a landlord, which is in effect a small business, entailing all sorts of legal responsibilities as well. There are two ways in which to earn profit with a buy-to-let property and they include Rental Yield and Capital Growth.

Rental yield is what your tenants pay in rent minus any expenses, such as, maintenance, running costs, repairs, and agents' fees. Capital growth occurs when you sell your buy-to-let property for more than you bought it for.

Rents <u>cannot always be guaranteed</u> due to fluctuations in the rental market, which may also include a period of time without paying tenants.

When house prices fall, then the value of your buy-to-let is likely to reduce as well, you may not be able to sell the property and if you do, you may not get as much for it as you had hoped for. However, on the flip side, when the rental market is good so are your profit margins and when house prices are soaring your return on investment, should you decide to sell, could be well worth the efforts of direct property investments.

Indirect Property Investment

An indirect property investment includes investing in property or real

Comparison table between direct and indirect property investing

Direct	Indirect
Tax relief	No tax relief
Large financial entry point	Smaller financial entry point
Varying timescales for return - generally longer	Varying timescales for return - generally shorter
Relatively low risk investment	Relatively low risk investment

estate, but without all the hands-on hassle. Ways in which this can be achieved is to invest in: property companies, bonds, peer-to-peer lending platforms, crowdfunding schemes, alongside other professional investors into an institution and Angel Investing (*see August edition article "What is an Angel Investor?"*).

When investing in this way, you would expect to receive a repayment schedule. A repayment schedule sets out in black and white exactly how your capital investment will be repaid, as well as how your potential interest will be paid. Depending on what style repayment schedule the party you invest into adopts, you may well discover that each schedule might look slightly different. For instance, some companies may have an 18-24 month rolling development term with target returns of 1.5 x investment.

Others may insist on a more regular approach where the investor receives a specified percentage and return of their total investment after a set number of months or years. Asset backed indirect property investments are regarded as being lower risk than direct property investment, and, it is important to note that there is still some level of risk in all investment strategies.

No matter where or how you invest there is never any guarantee that your investment capital will be returned or that a profit will be realized. The plus side to indirect property investment is that you don't always need a very large pot of spare cash to begin your investment journey.

It is always prudent to do your due diligence both on the type of investment strategy that suits your risk profile and on the people and or companies involved. Often the rewards far outweigh the risks when it comes to property investments whether direct or indirect.

Property investment, whether direct or indirect, is a solid and popular choice for many UK investors. Property always performs very well over the longer term and it is relatively easy to understand. In terms of developing an investment portfolio, property remains a key component for a sound and balanced strategy of investment.

Next month I will be discussing how to integrate property into your investment portfolio.

If you have found value in this article and want to discuss potential Angel Investment opportunities within the UK property market please contact Kirstie Shapiro at:

www.creativepropertypartners.com

Mobile: +44 (0) 7717 443 408

Kirstie Shapiro is Senior Managing Partner at Creative Property Partners, she helps Angel Investors to find the ideal properties within the UK Property Market to get the best returns on their financial investment.

Before starting her property partnership company, Kirstie worked for 8 years as a Private Personal Assistant to an eminent Cardiologist at the Royal Papworth Hospital in Cambridge UK and as an Actress and Model in her spare time.

After successfully enjoying property investment with her family, and encouraging others to develop their own property portfolios, Kirstie now advises people who have money that is sitting in the bank not earning decent interest rates, to partner with her as Angel Investors, investing in high return properties throughout the UK in major key cities.

kirstie@creativepropertypartners.com / P: +44 (0) 7717 443 408